The Time of Falling Apart

The Time of Falling Apart

poems

Wendy Donawa

HARBOUR PUBLISHING

Harbour Publishing Co. Ltd.
P.O. Box 219, Madeira Park, BC, V0N 2H0
www.harbourpublishing.com

Edited by Miriam Nichols
Cover photo by Ali Kazal
Cover and text design by Libris Simas Ferraz / Onça Publishing
Printed and bound in Canada
Printed on 100% recycled paper

Canada | Canada Council for the Arts | Conseil des arts du Canada
British Columbia Arts Council | British Columbia

Harbour Publishing acknowledges the support of the Canada Council for the Arts, the Government of Canada, and the Province of British Columbia through the BC Arts Council.

Library and Archives Canada Cataloguing in Publication
Title: The time of falling apart : poems / Wendy Donawa.
Names: Donawa, Wendy, author.
Identifiers: Canadiana (print) 20250211351 | Canadiana (ebook) 20250213508 | ISBN 9781998526307 (softcover) | ISBN 9781998526314 (EPUB)
Subjects: LCGFT: Poetry.
Classification: LCC PS8607.O64 T56 2025 | DDC C811/.6—dc23

Where are we moored?
What are the bindings?
What behooves us?

from *An Atlas of the Difficult World*, Adrienne Rich.

Table of Contents

That Sensible Planning-Ahead Thing

Did they wonder: How did we come to this?

Wendy Donawa

That Sensible Planning-Ahead Thing

On Thursday last my love and I drove north to Sidney to prepay our cremations.
Odd, you might think, and we did too, and sat in the parking lot laughing
nervously.

The day was fine, salty breezes off the water, Magritte clouds dotting the sky.
We congratulated ourselves we'd done that sensible planning-ahead thing.

Enough parental dramas where nobody knew where the papers were.
Or claims from obscure nephews with bad hair and pocket-protectors.

We walked through the hardware store's garden supply yard.
Finally found the office, its large tortoiseshell cat presiding.

The manager breezed in, windblown from her bike ride.
Our fears of Dickensian lugubriousness uncalled for.

It was all as sensible as sorting potatoes. The cat mounted the desk
and glared at us throughout. We knew glibness would be uncalled for.

She gave us to-do lists and price lists and lists of all the people she'd call.
It was entirely satisfactory, and the cat purred when we left.

Then we felt slightly hysterical and went to a French bistro.
We downed grilled cheese sandwiches dripping with Gruyère and
caramelized onions.

Stabilized over a bottle of Pinot Noir, my true love said,
Well, the one who's left will know what to do. Then we cried again.

Eros and Thanatos on our seesaw, she said, and we laughed,
then took Highway 17 home, into the rest of our lives.

The Wolf in Me

Before the war, Dad saw a pretty teacher, was dumbstruck with love.
Post-war I came aboard, inherited his surname: *Love*.

They named me *Wendy* after she of Peter Pan so famed.
Such king-and-country anglophiles, all things Brit they loved.

At school we learned to print, proud chalking up our blackboard names;
I came to hate the playground's teasing singsong chants of *love, love, love*.

At high school, courage, high romance of classics stuffed my brain.
My name lacked *gravitas*, a sentimental pastel Hallmark Love.

(Just now, a fat red-throated finch has landed on my window frame
and, rash seducer, pours forth trills and warbles to his love.)

With college, etymology. I found ancestral history in my name;
Not soppy sentimental love, but Celtic roots of *louve*,

the female wolf. I thought of forefolk to the Scottish north, untamed
as they repelled invading woad-stained Britons; came to love

my name, a tribe of power, and was happy to explain
my wolf-self—but fate intervened; I fell in love

and somehow lost my lupine fierceness, left my name
to take on *Donawa*, and follow my beloved

to islands roiled with history as they spurned colonial chains,
but rich with heat and rain and energies I came to love,

though when I looked up *Donawa*, one site said *No meaning found*. In vain
I sought another: *Origin unknown*. A US census strove

to show this name occurs just once a million; claimed
that of these few, 71 per cent were Black. There was no love

in this, the sort of thing that country will maintain
though Trinidad now shows a plentiful array of

Donawas. Where is the wolf in me to howl against the erasure bane?
Throughout the Eastern Caribbean, Donawas love

to roam, take root, recolonize the hearts of those who claim,
as you do, Donawa, so far north, that any ground is home for love.

Small Boys in Sailor Suits

The photo's faded, brown, 1910, I'd guess. Faux drapes signal respectability.
No one smiles except my irrepressible four-year-old mother, a blur
clamped to Grandad's stern knee, her placid twin melded to Grandmama's.
Behind the squirming twins, the glum pubescent eldest.
In front, Gordon, the serious sailor-suited boy.
Somewhere, the first Gordie's ghost has drifted from the Cayley churchyard,
from the frigid prairie homestead where he coughed his life away,
where they left him when they pushed west until there was no more West.

The pivot, the small death of *Now*. Did they wonder: *how did we come to this?*

British Grandmama: respectable family, small means, poor prospects,
waded the shallow matrimonial pool, then chose a dashing tradesman,
unthinkable, no gentleman. Setting sail for the colonies, any colonies,
they'd populate the New World's *terra nullius*
—there's no one home, so we'll take the house.

Victoria: seething with gold miners, second sons,
disgraced nephews, speculators.
Grandad builds a small sturdy home, middle class signifier,
but hauls massive horse-drawn stone blocks
for breakwater construction. If asked,
the children are to say
He works for the city.

No one questions whose lands they've displaced,
whose fisheries and forests, whose sacred sites despoiled,
whose children abducted, whose graveyards.

Streets are paved, church steeples rise,
and families pose for portraits with lace-shawled wives,
small boys in sailor suits.

Leaving Pendergast

Of that brown-shingled house on Pendergast
my pre-school memories are vague, dream-like
the kitchen   *dark*   *smells I can't name*   *baby yelling in the crib*
small stove-side scenarios
        I'm being bathed in the sink.
        I'm not to pick raisins from the porridge to eat first
        nor scrape and suck brown sugar's melting sprinkle.
Then, morning's bundled-up ejection to the urchin street,
its coal-fire smoke and squabble   girls have to be bad guys
when we play war   holler rude words   climb forbidden junk piles.
Iceman's clop-clopping horse leaves dung to throw or stamp
until we hear our whistle   *short short long*
each mother has a different riff to reel us in.

Big brother   another species   lurks with his own kind,
their secret maps and hideouts.
Here's Mr. Lee Jin's rickety vegetable truck   fake threats
to cart me off in his big woven basket.
Mum gives him cigarettes at Christmas,
wraps them in silver paper.

Auntie lives up the block, Mum's identical twin sister;
my cousin and I share a birthday too, and so
will two yet-unborn siblings. Fierce tribal loyalties
roar up and down the boulevard. We don't think much about
our doubled lives.

Sometimes our Mums show us pictures of the little princesses,
help us mark xx on the calendar for when the dads come home.
We hope they can stay with the king if they like   but they turn up here
scratchy chins   thumping boots   shouty voices,
we hatch treasonous plots to find faraway wars for them
        but they just stay and stay.

(In half a century I'll revisit Pendergast   the old house has been lifted
squared and trimmed   architected   into upscale condo flats
chic urban garden.)

Dad stays but Uncle takes his family to Australia.
Uncle says   *Never marry a twin*
you only get half a person.

Our brown house rents for fifteen dollars a month   and Dad says
may as well put that toward our own house. I don't know
what it means to put money toward. Maybe like with Art, who is blind
and runs the corner store with Neapolitan ice cream for Sunday
and when you buy something
you have to put money toward him so he can find it.

So Dad buys a new brown house   real fridge not an icebox
real furnace not a sawdust hopper
and hot air comes up through the grate
where my little brother and I sleep in the ell of the eaves.
Mr. Lee Jin doesn't come any more.

Big brother sleeps in his basement room by the furnace
He doesn't have a twin cousin   Does this make him so sad?
He comes in late at night, smells funny. Sometimes he shouts in the basement.
I'm getting big, don't pay attention   thinking about art school.
He leaves school early. Gets a jalopy. Mum cries when he leaves home
and for a while we get postcards. Then nothing. Then the call
the police regret to inform

                                        grief suffocates the brown house
and I take off for Real Life in Vancouver, wondering if
I should have gone down to the basement when he yelled.

I still wonder.

My grandson is his age now.

Gemini Terribiles

They must each have had names, but I only recall
the Terrible Winterbottom Twins. And Mr. Bell,
his war-addled brain. Compulsive accounts of
his war-hero brother, shot down, torso severed.
We ten-year-olds, pitiless, snorted,
rolled eyes, retched and gagged
'til he spun round to stare at our blank guilty faces
and shouted, poor Gollum, or, frenzied,
stalked desk rows with the wide wood ruler
hauled culprits up front, bent them over his desk
and whacked.

Once a twin hatched
a prank so egregious,
he hauled her up front, bent her over the desk,
began whacking. A WonderGirl flash,
her twin flew through air onto Mr. Bell's back
wrapped her legs round his waist, clutched his throat,
clung, a *Chrysochus auratus* beetle, iridescent with fury.

Dread rhythm that day from the strap at The Office.
Rare punishment, kept for tough boys who broke windows.
And the silence. No wails from the twins.

Then we moved; I changed schools.

Time to time, I imagine them,
Artful Dodgers with petty crime empires,
fast learners who never get caught.
Pretty girls, ruthless, finessed up the ladder,
"protectors" who fund them,
for law school, wealth management, one for each twin.
Drive Porsches, wear Prada, Armani, Versace,
flash Rolexes, terrors to all who oppose,
perhaps running for office,
iridescent with diamonds and malice,
gemini terribiles.

Shame

Look thy last on all things lovely, quavered poor Miss Turpin,
sparrow-boned Miss Turpin, smocked, bunned.
High-strung, high-minded, she strove to foist
her missionary zeal for poetry
upon graceless grade 10s, heathens
as we all were, ungrateful, feral with hormones and energy.
Some of the worst boys would come early
and bang chalkboard brushes together
to induce her paroxysms of coughing
as she entered. We didn't all join them.

We didn't stop them either.

Till to delight thou have paid thy utmost blessing . . .
(memorizing that old chestnut for homework)
And why indeed would we embrace the fleeting transient loveliness
she wished on the feckless young, whose *utmost blessing* was fleshed out
in the jalopy's back seat at Friday night's drive-in?

Two years on, a few got pregnant, a few were expelled,
some left to work in their dad's machine shop. A few caught the poetry bug.
A few had veneers of civility, even embryonic consciences.
Miss Turpin was long retired; we'd hardly noticed
her delicate spectral presence
even when she was there.

Daniel (no longer a chalkboard banger) and I,
both summoned to the principal's office, told
of Miss Turpin's mysterious unnameable illness,
directed (we two, her old students) to visit, represent the school.
Setting off on the bus, some eye-rolling snickers
at this unrequested Florence Nightingale role
until the thin tinkle of her doorbell and her tremulous greeting.

She lived with a sister as fragile as she,
and poured tea into cups so delicate it seemed they might shatter
as easily as their owners. The very air was threadbare.

I do not remember the conversation, only that
I flooded hot with shame to realize
they were afraid of us,

and on the returning bus, we avoided each other's eyes
and did not speak all the way home.

The Summit

The Arctic front's tide surges in from the bay
across Dallas Road, which ribbons all along the coast,
a deluge flooding Ross Bay Cemetery,
and I'm minded of childhood's storms so violent
they swept logs over the breakwater onto the old graveyard,
its underground city of Victorian worthies. Shrouds of snow
fling themselves at still-standing monuments:
angels, cherubs, the more eminent citizens
and wives they lost, successively, to childbirth.

Blizzardy winds hurl spumes of spray house-high along Dallas
to sluice down Earl Street, Moss Street, Linden, Cook, where, melting,
they will quickly plug the drains, pour into basements,
disrupt retired lawyers' model train collections,
saturate the green shag carpets of proud rec rooms,
and inundate malls, their hardware stores and disconsolate bakeries,
their pubs blinking *Open Open Open* as snow piles up
and everywhere sump pumps throb
like a great suburban heart.

Snow obliterates Clover Point, once a destination to park
and tussle with fast boys, keeping an eye out for cops
who might tap the window and ask how old we were.
Breakers crest and foam across the Ogden Point breakwater,
obscuring its Coast Salish murals,
tilting houseboats rakishly at Fisherman's Wharf,
while freezing blasts have strung long icy drips
from the august bronze noses of
Queen Victoria and Emily Carr.

Curtains of snow veil Beacon Hill's summit, one-time military lookout
for the Pacific's coastal traffic, and long before that,
First Nations nearby farmed its slopes with camas bulbs
bartered on inland waterways
or up the coast, braving autumn gales,
Each spring, the hillside floods indigo
with camas blossoms rippling like another sea
and old men smoke on benches at the summit
above the prickly undergrowth where I first
lay down with a Trinidadian boy
so beautiful I married him.

Pas de Deux

How My Parents Reacted to Me

Modest, their anglophile customs and certainties.
Innocent foot-soldiers, settlers for Empire.

Toasted the Queen with each Christmas dinner.
Scrapbooks to cut out and paste little Royals.

My flouting convention confused and alarmed them,
pretty pink socks, little lockets to tame me.

How they hoped a respectable boy would engage me.
A bank clerk, perhaps civil service, solidity.

Speechless at first when they met my intended.
But rallied, made tea in the best silver teapot.

Put a brave face on my flight to Barbados.
Each week sent love in a blue tissue aerogram.

How I Reacted to My Parents

Bored by their care, their predictable niceness
Scornful of all that was snug, post-war cozy.

Disdaining the replica life that they wished for me,
shocked them with strange words: *resistance, angst, gender*.

Black jeans and turtleneck, thought it looked edgy,
art school nonchalance, paint under fingernails,

candles in wine bottles, urbane pretensions,
life-modelling, rented that basement, so arty.

Hitchhiked and met the dark prince of my fancies,
swiftly got rid of my cumbersome virginity.

Chose a new life and decamped for Barbados,
where I was the stranger and longed for my mother.

To My Hand by Happenstance

The man on the top of the mountain did not fall there
reads the strip from my fortune cookie,
banal, but I'd felt like something crunchy.
Heard an echoing crunch and
found my ivory *netsuke* in two pieces underfoot.
Finger-length—I'd crushed its fragile mid-point
where hand-carved threads screwed, unscrewed
this small, robed man, his face tranquil.

In toddler days I played under the kitchen table,
was allowed, if it rained, Mother's button box,
Grandad's bag of Chinese coins—some square, some perforated—
allowed to unscrew—gently, gently—this manikin.

Fast forward to my three decades
in the Caribbean, where years cycled
between rainy season—thick steamy air
when everything swelled, doors jammed and stuck—
then dry season, so desiccant our skin itched,
wood split, sun the enemy. Among my nostalgia trinkets,
fine cracks traced the ivory knick-knack.

No more than the man on the mountaintop
did this carving come to my hand by happenstance.
I never questioned when I could, and now there is no one to ask.
My motley ancestors, second sons, disappointing nephews
scattered, not leaders of men, the heft and slog
of their hardscrabble lives, machinery of empire,
and yet, their bone-deep belief in Britannia, its rule, its waves
and all that. *Colonizing, what colonizing?* they'd have said,
themselves both colonized and colonizing,
tossing small coins to sweating porters,
to laundresses squatting by tubs,
to an artisan bent over his bench,
his miniscule knives, gouges, scraps of ivory.

How frangible the robe's edges,
etched ridges, darkened patina.
Its crushed sash now a strip of cello tape.

Not in the Same Way

She was about nine, she told us,
when she and her little friend got naked.
Being a pious child and afraid of the eternal,
also a clever child who loved long words,
she confessed to the priest she'd committed adultery.

When we stopped laughing, we wondered why
so many of our bookish pals, mainly atheists,
are lapsed Catholics, or, like me,
arisen from the high church Anglican featherbed,
where you get all the bells and smells, the poetics,
but not so much damnation.

I often find myself returning to these protocols
and wonder why I can't quite shake them off,
wonder why yoga, tai chi, a great book club,
and sound Left politics
don't plug the gap.
Arcane rituals indelible as curry stains
on my dark November heart.

I believe
that the sun is a huge ball of electrically charged hot gas
and that the earth orbits it every year.
And I believe
that Bus 24 will stop across the street
as I brew my morning coffee.
But not in the same way.

And not in the way that
when I walk the path along the inlet
on a foggy morning, I will encounter
pyracantha, rosehips, snowberries'
soft shine through the shifting mist.

I said "arcane" with condescending scorn,
although some proscriptions are
sensible as traffic lights. Required days of rest, for instance,
more needed now than ever, in this online moment
and its home offices, their schizoid business jackets
over PJ pants, and Skip the Dishes.
Isn't it nice to set all that down for a day?
And tithing, which, when compassion and generosity
have hit *delete*, is a hard act to recover.
And what about *custody of the tongue*,
which, taken seriously, might avert much marital damage,
also pogroms, massacres, and the odd guided missile.

But the only all-seeing entity I can get my head around
is the whirling algorithm—its sinister constellation of factoids—
although not in the same God-ish way
as the liturgical language I term *sacred*
for the cadence of the King James version
that comes in the night and hums in my mind
as I struggle with a poem. Oh,
keep me as an apple of thine eye; hide me under the shadow of thy wing.

And I recall my child-self on a sunrise beach
listening to the tide's pebbly click and shush
and crows cawing in the arbutus,
when I first thought *Holy*.

I believe
kindness and intelligence
as essential in the public lives of governments
as in friendships and their intimacies.
But I believe also
that malice and self-interest are tireless, protean,
their powerful muscle of Intention restless and inventive.
How to hold both?

I believe
our wretched species has run out of time,
fouled its nest beyond salvation.
But once, silent hours long past the time
my beloved should have been
delivered to me from surgery, I murmured
please God pleasegodpleasegodplease . . .

Still, the inlet's ebb tide pulls sunlight down to the harbour.
And once I saw a full moon rise from the east
while the sun stood its copper disk
on the western horizon's shelf
and for a moment, the world held them both.

Cullet

. . . non-refundable glass containers will be ground down into small pieces called "cullet" and used in the manufacturing of a variety of things such as fiberglass insulation, sandblasting material and even sand for golf-course sand-traps. Ground glass can also be added to asphalt in the making of new roads.

Recycling notice from the council of the Dockside Green
Condo Association

The notice cheered me up as I sorted the week's recycling,
scrubbed marmalade and peanut butter jars, milk and wine bottles
to become cullet in their new life, useful,
expiate their contaminating potential.
It was restful to imagine them as insulation or asphalt,
a regeneration of productive life, a humble immortality, salvation even

but that's because the CBC was playing Bach's Mass in G minor
as I tied off the recycle sack and started on the paper,
shredded documents, stacked newspapers,
deconstructed wine boxes
even emptied a waste basket of used Kleenex
although that's cheating a bit but surely all might be
in a state of grace, delivered from environmental sin
which made me think of the cullet of my unrecycled life,
its small envies and meanesses committed or suspected
or resented, but Bach always gets me in the back brain
and the problem is, once you've believed in transcendence
it's hard to live without it.

A thread of something settles, just below my conscious life,
where I lie in wait like fishers submerging their slow arms
to tickle fishes' bellies, gently capture them, and bring them to the air.
The words emerge then. Something comes, analogous to prayer,
a transformation crafts the cullet of our lives
to poems, to beating wings of swans,
to meteors' gold scribble on the ceiling of the night.

Why I Didn't Pick Up a Latte and Croissant for Breakfast

walk the shoreline at first light   you will see
across the waterway   how rays of lavender, peach, pewter
coat the skyline's concrete geometry   the gravel pit
even the slope of the contaminated soil dump
(its embankments rehabilitated   pristine   they say)
small day-glo waves ride an early tide up the inlet
past the rapids   kingfishers flash blue praise
tranquil ducks paddle water meadows
while great blue herons dart and gobble
and all this watery realm sings creation

before mists lift   imagine the great canoes   cedar,
that loaded their harvest to trade up the coast

see how the littoral's bushes sag with blackberries   rosehips,
crabapples   here you will also find the young man who
rocks back and forth   sobs inconsolably
for the shredded possessions on his tattered blanket
weeping   he holds them up one by one   puts them down
what's his story?   he's not saying   the rehabilitated dump
camouflages mortals in their gimcrack tents
they move slowly   sullen   wondering if today
the cops and dogs will arrive   move them along

Reversal

(Variation after Warsan Shire's palindrome "Backwards")

If only she wouldn't phone at 2:00 a.m.
I could write her back into her cottage,
whipping up eggs for a soufflé, Vivaldi blasting,
sunset gin and tonic under the plum tree.
But she wonders why she's living in *this* place,
meals provided, adequate, she says, but
not to her standard. Her dinner companions
poor conversationalists. Says she has nothing
she looks forward to. If we could write her back
into her contralto solos, her *a cappella* choir . . .
If casserole-bearing neighbours, concerned,
had not forced her winter door, reported her collapse,
then ambulance attendants would not say
she can't come back here.
Casserole-bearing neighbours
would be welcomed in, sit at the kitchen table
while she lights candles, opens a good red.
Then the hospital would not say *malnutrition, disorientation,*
systemic infections; specialists would not say,
You cannot return to your home. Neighbours might have
a welcome-home happy hour, and they'd laugh
about her ambulance adventure.
Cleaning companies would not refuse to enter her home.
The bathroom walls, black with mould,
would return to the crisp white and blue
I painted as her birthday present
some golden summer ago. The leaking fridge,
its rank cargo of vegetable decay, sour milk,
would return, pristine, with market carrots,
fresh greens, a small succulent chicken
and rows of jewel-hued preserves on the sunny windowsill.

The cairn of gin bottles would disappear, reveal a gleaming kitchen floor.
The mice would leave, return to fields and grassy burrows.
Mouse nests behind the walls, the gnawed wiring
in cupboards, and in shoes and bags.
Fetid sheets would whisk through laundry cycles,
returning themselves, warm and folded, to their shelves,
if only she wouldn't phone at 2:00 a.m.

If only she wouldn't phone at 2:00 a.m.,
returning themselves, warm and folded, to their shelves,
fetid sheets would whisk again through laundry cycles.
In cupboards and in shoes and bags,
mouse nests; behind the walls, gnawed wiring.
Mice would leave, return to fields and grassy burrows,
would disappear, reveal a gleaming kitchen floor,
a sunny windowsill, no cairn of gin bottles,
but rows of jewel-hued preserves.
Fresh greens, a small succulent chicken
would not decay to rank cargo,
no sour milk, no leaking fridge.
Since that golden summer ago,
walls, painted as her birthday present,
would return to their crisp white and blue.
If bathroom walls weren't black with mould,
cleaning companies would not refuse to enter.
About her ambulance adventure,
a welcome-home happy hour? They'd laugh:
You cannot return to your home. Neighbours wouldn't fear
systemic infections if specialists did not say,
then the hospital would not say, *malnutrition, disorientation.*
Meanwhile she dreams candles, opening a good red,
a welcome seat at the kitchen table,
if casserole-bearing neighbours did not say

She can't come back here.
Then ambulance attendants would not say,
would not have forced her winter door, reported her collapse,
if casserole-bearing neighbours concerned.
Her contralto solo, her *a cappella* choir
she looked forward to . . . If we could write her back . . .
Poor conversationalist, says she has nothing.
Not to her standard, her dinner companions.
Meals provided, adequate, she says, but
she wonders why she's living in this place,
no sunset gin and tonic under the plum tree,
no whipping up eggs for a soufflé, Vivaldi blasting.

Could we write her back to her cottage?
If only she wouldn't phone at 2:00 a.m.

Who Hasn't Leaned Over the Bridge Rail, Beguiled

by black and silver currents tugging the moon, how its star-filled deeps
feed our hypnotic illusion that
the bridge slides over an immobile tide?
Who hasn't wondered in an idle way or a desperate one
if happiness is that unstable   or that illusory
or maybe we don't have a word for it,
when we have done the right things, washed weekend cars,
filed our tax on time, gone to parent-teacher meetings,
voted and recycled; still, the happiness we *deserve*—a chimera.

All mammals build and fight, mate and breed in their seasons.
None but we feel *entitled* to happiness, its Norse root: *hap*, means *chance*, *luck*.
We pack the picnic, and it rains; woo the beloved, who leaves;
take vitamins but get early dementia.
Who hasn't leaned over the bridge rail   beguiled
by its winking black and silver invitation?

Pleasure is different. Its roots travel well,
from the Latin *placere, affording satisfaction*, to Old French *plaisir*,
while the late 14th century defined *pleasure* as *discretion*, *will* and *desire*.
Those ancestors hoped for eternal happiness,
having given up on earthly possibilities—though surely they too hoped
their families would not die in the plague, their daughters not be raped
or their sons flogged. Hoped the landlord would not burn their huts,
and that the cow would breed again.

But we with twice their lifespan don't wait for the hereafter,
live long enough to use will and desire for our pleasure
to forage those rain-forest chanterelles off the highway
watch sunrise burn mist from the Gorge
treasure the loving-kindness of friends, make poems
and cherish mornings   the young barista takes pains
to make a perfect design on the foam of my latte
although then he clips on the lid.

The Morning After His Funeral

I'd already packed my bags; Mum spoke little. Our last breakfast together, toast in the old toaster with its flap-down sides, preserves from the gnarled peach tree espaliered on the sunny wall by the back door. From time to time, I reached to hold her hands. Her Parkinson's tremor. "We had forty-eight years of love," she said. "But his pain . . . If I could bring him back tomorrow, I wouldn't."

late bees tunnel
in fallen peaches—
too late to harvest

That Conjured Last Day

How can I imagine earth's last day
without *relinquish relinquish relinquish*
Who might I be without all that I can touch hold
my love waking warm from sleep?
Where is delight when the gone-ness of Yo Yo Ma,
the not-there of finches' return who nest, noisy and cheerful,
who make music daily perch on the balcony's metal heron singing
and shitting, singing and shitting down the tempered steel feathers
Oh how I love the world's *thing*-ness!

Oddly, in that conjured last day
I feel remote, and strangely calm
whether from some psychochemical assist
or mysterious enhancement of my own spirit
I cannot say. But I have relinquished vain regrets: some minor
like the guitar I vowed to learn, still languishing in my cupboard,
some vast my son's long silence intractable.
But not the terror I expected,
as when I first heard "invasive carcinoma"
or when I spent two hours circling in the small plane
that finally crash-landed.

So that day I wake to stars in their spheres singing
in heaven's river my lover's soft breathing until she wakes,
until the first eastern glow grows a blessing of sunburst.
Without haste we dress grind coffee beans
take steaming cups to the balcony. The finches are already at it.
What miracle manifests in my favourite mug,
its heavy ceramic heft heating cupped hands,
that fragrance? Oh relinquish! Can I?
I have relinquished, for this time, the need to write cheques,
complete that course, finish the Ferrante Quartet,
return library books empty the compost. On this day
gone the need for apologies or invitations.

We don't talk much stroll along the inlet.
A few quiet watercraft moored or adrift
but none of them look like Charon's dark skiff
or Lawrence's ship of death with its *little cakes*.
Nor is this brackish stream the River Styx.

Mysterium Tremendum

They phoned me to say I should come
and come soon if I wanted to see him
since all the signs showed he was *actively dying.*
This seemed such a strange phrase,
as though set for a final performance,
which perhaps it was. A grim script

for the man that I'd loved through my green years,
his fine warm skin now grey and mottled and cold,
hands and feet cyanotic, his spirit gone travelling.
Rasping breaths we aligned with our breaths
as we do when we know they're preparing to leave us,
as though this will hold them aloft.

But what if that distance is only a focus
on destinations we cannot know
until, perhaps, we arrive there ourselves?
Our voices left on the wharf while the vessel
navigates toward a great absence, *mysterium tremendum.*
Aristotle believed the soul to be
that which makes the living thing alive,
used different words for live body and dead.

When childhood's conceptual wiring hatched,
I learned to read Dick and Jane's
monosyllabic world: *See Spot run. Oh oh oh.*
That was then. Now six-year-olds in nearby schools
discuss the nature of animate beings,
discern that they move, eat, have babies,
and that things that don't do this are not alive.

Perhaps *active dying* is not a misnomer.
Maybe dying is as onerous as getting born,
those hours working through uncanny transformations.
Maybe one is as numinous as the other,
but no one can tell us of either.

Fearful at the evening window, my small son
dreamed a being he called the Hunjer
that would come for him in the night.
I scoured the grassy landscape for the Hunjer
and finally saw a tree burnt black against the sky.

Its arm-like branches reached with terrible claws
that twitched and shuddered in the wind.
You see, he said, *It's alive*
and it's coming for me.

Scorch of Time

It's almost November, light dwindling, and the last gold leaves
flare against cedar, against time for the melancholy tasks
that trim our diminishing lives. That edgy little condo
with the steel ladder to its loft is history,
but even in our present digs we're overwhelmed
with goods and chattels, treasures from passed chapters.
A constant book-exodus to the Little Free Libraries
but books seem to breed when we're not looking.
Aunties' gifts of jewellery I never wore, will never wear,
no takers for now-tarnished silver cutlery they assembled
fork by fork to promote my marriageability.

St. Jerome kept a skull on his desk to remind him all is vanity,
but the self-portrait I painted as I turned thirty
flaunts *the righteousness I had before the scorch of time.*
That girl's level stare confronts onlookers.
She could take on the world. She'll have had a place in art history.
She bought a used Vespa for ninety dollars and covered the metropole,
grabbed the world's here and now. *I miss who I was.*
Now *impatience bows in service to another story.*

Drowned out by the *ars poetica*
of letters to the newspapers deploring bike lanes, immigrants, public art,
peevish diatribes convinced civilization is threatened
by the misuse of *lie* and *lay*.
Hungry ghosts, you will never have enough.
Always you will stay late in the office.
No one awaits your return with delight.

Heading home, I'll pick up flowers for her.
Chrysanthemums, asters, a riot of dahlias.

Between Ground and Feast

Between
the ground and the feast is where I live now.

Ada Limón

The Time of Falling Apart

I'm a dragon woman, born in a dragon year
and by the zodiac's account, I should be
tenacious, confident, powerful, generous.
Lucky, too. Should marry rat, monkey, or rooster.
Sadly, this year's zodiac is less optimistic.
I am opposed by Tai Sui, god of age,
who foresees an overall lack of good luck,
the outlook for my health also unfortunate
as I approach the time of falling apart.

Some of my losses are careless, rather than tragic:
I lose my glasses before finding them on my head
and have lost enough hearing to embarrass myself regularly.
But what other deserters have left my memory palace?
What of my keys, grocery lists, important dates,
the name of that nice woman in the blue shirt,
the best way through East Van, my favourite socks?
Self-pruning, fruit reduces its pull-force
so it falls away easily, energies no longer required.
How is it that I who careened merrily
across two provinces, three mountain ranges
to meet my lover,
now avoid night driving, parallel parking?

In pools of crystalizing snow, these sodden Garry oak leaves.
I'm drawn to winter branches, their spareness and latency.

If you look past the oak's roots,
up its gnarled bark corrugations, its lichen armour,
past its branches' baroque skew, stub of an amputated limb
in its cozy sleeve of moss, past a fretwork of twigs,
you might fall up into the sky.

Frilly white barnacles of lichen.
Burying my hands in mossy ruffles,
I remember running my fingers
through my son's springy hair.
I flatline to think of it.

The year's nights draw in
and veins of leaves close like blocked arteries.
Their barrier of thin-walled cells
whose purpose it is to break down in autumn
as it approaches the time of falling apart,
as it invites abscission, the separation of stem from leaf,
of horn from skull, of claw, husk;
also from those who renew themselves seasonally,
salamanders shed body parts to shun predation,
or those who'd rather sacrifice a breast
than yield it prey to a malignancy.

Some years ago in Cowichan Valley,
A Quw'utsun Elder, master carver, explained
near-final stages of a pole he'd made.
Power: its carved and sombre range of mythic predators.
Before we left, he asked quietly, *What is your predator?*
Before we left, we held hands, he said a prayer.
I'd just had my diagnosis two days before.

The oak's twiggy black canopy engraves a wintery sky,
all *grisaille* reflections over the inlet's glossy mirror
where doubled ducks confer cordially
over the long Vs of their contrails.

Duplex: Glean

The sun will set, whether we watch or not.
Whether or not we see those men in night's dusk.

In night's dusk, the men we see gleaning a dumpster
seem tranquil as Millet's *Angelus*,

tranquil as angels, grateful for millet.
A ruckus! A murder of crows, their caws,

their cause their fledgling, a hawk's murderous need.
But don't we all rend and tear to survive?

Rend and tear, survival, even if it's
only a dearth of toilet paper.

Toilet paper, a dearth? I'd choose
the raptor's honest, if ravenous, necessity,

and those men's rapt necessity: to glean, ravenous,
whether or not we see them as the sun sets.

Online Poetry Workshop in the Plague Year

A Zoom-quilt of poets,
we strive to bring these squares
into alignment.

We're together; we're not together,
we're on coasts that frame the continent,
salt air our element.

It's a time-space continuum.
One watches night slide over the prairie.
One's just finished supper; another yawns; it's midnight.

One lives in my neighbourhood
near the inlet's muscular tides,
bright shuttle of kayaks: scarlet, yellow.

Others speak of babies in safe rooms,
of the iceman dug from a glacier,
poignancy of his gopher-skin coat.

One remembers my cousin, dying,
her burgeoning garden, fervent with growth.
Her old ginger cat.

Grandma crocheted strips to frame her patchwork quilts.
We tried to match the squares. Sturdy stuff:
tweed, cotton, denim, corduroy.

Pandemic Blues

That next-door lock clicks   her cat's got out again
Yeah, it clicks alright   the woman's cat's got out again.
There it is   its world and its disdain.

its world's a condo corridor   a dusty wilderness beyond
yeah, dusty carpet too   a wilderness beyond
cat-food dish   litterbox   Escapes any second,

and there the woman crouches   makes small pleading noises
Yeah, she jingles toys and makes small pleading noises
She's tossing chicken shreds   nearer   nearer the decoys.

The cat retreats   licks paws and stares with scorn
Don't want that jingle toy   it stares with scorn
It wants that stalk and lunge   the glory of bright gore.

At last it's bored   it's regal with contempt   returns
It's bored at last and regal with contempt   returns
the woman weeps a little   turns

and clicks the door closed   draws evening curtains
yeah, she clicks that lock and draws those evening curtains.
Staring into the fridge   as if she's sure
the answer's in its veggie drawer.

Lessons From the Silver Screen

I grew up with movies that taught me the meek
might inherit a white picket fence of
mid-century bliss, a green velour lawn
Dick and Jane, even dumb Baby Sally
could romp on; matched lampstands, twin beds
from which Rock and Doris (or was it Tony)
bid goodnight, chastely bed-robed?
They taught me twin-sets and pearls,
the perky bow that welcomed hubby home.
All this might be mine if I played my cards right.

Although Annie got her gun, she learned
you can't get a man with a gun. Movies stressed
that girls who wear glasses do not get a pass,
nor apprentice to marry millionaires.
Movies advised me to smile though your heart is breaking
while grade nine mean girls got asked to the prom,
went home with lipstick smeared and
sweaters inside out. At the wallflower table,
I smiled behind Coke-bottle glasses,
poured fruit punch for horny boys who thought
there is nothing like a dame.
I began to doubt that someday
my prince would come and even
English 91 taught us the pattern set by patient Griselda
ever since Penelope sewed a fine seam. Then ripped it out.

Vermeer's *Milkmaid*

(After Johannes Vermeer's *The Milkmaid*, c. 1660)

Desire pervades everything, nothing human can be cleansed of it.
Its roots from the Latin *desiderare*, to long for,
suggest these longings as a form of energy,
even destiny.

For instance, a desire to make boeuf bourguignon
for the one you love. Even while shopping, its destiny unfolds:
pig's foot to enrich the sauce, pork belly you'll slice in matchsticks,
its rendered fat to caramelize mushrooms, sear pearl onions.
Collagen-rich short rib crusting brown in fat and butter.
A weighty Burgundy. Then the long slow simmer. The waiting.

Vermeer's desires manifested in his pigments. Meticulous grinding
of indigo, red madder, copper green, lead tin yellow, verdigris,
lead white with its subtle undertones, ultramarine from precious lapis lazuli.
Schiele's much-desired, arsenic-filled green (also used to poison rats)
sickened artists through the ages. To this day, nothing embraces the senses
like Vermeer's translucent glazes. His invented concave mirrors
enlarge his ravenous gaze. His wondrous ochres, cadmium yellows
flood cool pale sunlight through the casement window, numinous
across the young maid's serene brow, her steady gaze, firm grasp
as she pours a stream of milk into a pottery bowl. You could reach out
and grasp her arm, its smooth skin, blood coursing beneath,
those supple bones steadying an exquisite stream of
poisonous white lead milk that froths eternally
into its bowl.

Ortolans

(after *The Dance Class* and *Woman at Her Bath* by Edgar Degas, 1873–1876)

In case you're wondering,
I'm the chunky one up on the left,
glad of a chance to rest my ruined feet
while the old man drones on, cantankerous
about our pliés, arabesques, attitudes.
How he loves the sound of his voice,
while his old buddies, roués,
eminent patrons, fine gentlemen,
stare at bare legs, fantasize, make plans.
Really, I don't know how many years I've got left
in the game, and is this any better than
bending over laundry tubs or being groped in taverns?

I make a little extra, modelling for him,
in case you're wondering. I'm the one
in *Woman at Her Bath*. I've got a name, you know,
a face too, if he cared to make a painting *about* a woman.
But it's all about him. Considering *woman as an animal*,
cheap bugger didn't even send for warm water
while he took a break, chatted up his patrons.
I waited, shivering, perched on the bath's chilly rim.
Critics gush about *the natural gesture, the flow of light across the body*,
and even I see magic in his pigments,
the startling light, the breathing ribcage,
water sliding wonderfully down my back.

And now he's drilling *les petits rats*, new to the *corps de ballet*.
Kids really, some of them join us at ten, twelve,
nimble street urchins eager to enter
a state of enchantment, applause, pretty costumes.
Behind frothy artifice, tawdry finery,
a brothel culture in the alcoves.
I was a *petit rat*. I was nine.

Paunchy gentlemen murmur, breathe heavily.
Patrons anticipate *droit de seigneur*, a quite different *pas de deux*.
How they long to please, *les petits rats*,
Bending, splaying, springing on their little bird legs.
Poor little *ortolans*.

In case you're wondering,
the ortolan is a small songbird, now rare,
reserved for royal gourmands, the stinking rich, the eminent.

Here's what happens. First, blind the bird.
Confine it with plentiful grain, to gorge and fatten.
Drown it in brandy; leave it there to marinate.
Finally, roast the tiny corpse; present it with ceremony.
The bird is eaten whole under a large linen napkin
the patron has draped over his head
to savour the aromas or, others say,
to hide the shame from God. I wouldn't know.

Ah now, those poppets, how they flounce and pirouette.

Hold the bird by the beak, eat the thing whole, chomp
the twiggy feet, hot gush of gut and fat, crunch of skull
(like tiny bone-cracks, working *en pointe* far too young).
Those who have experienced this ritual
report an intense and complex pleasure,
positively orgasmic.

They say it makes them quite faint to remember.
I wouldn't know.
In case you're wondering.

Dukkha (1)

½ c hazelnuts
¼ c sesame seeds
2 tbsp coriander seeds
1 tbsp cumin seeds
1 tbsp fennel seeds
2 tsp black peppercorns
1 tsp fine sea salt

Preheat oven 350°C.

Place nuts on small baking tray 6–7 minutes, until golden brown.

Wrap in clean towel and rub vigorously to remove loose skins.

Transfer to plate to cool.

Place sesame seeds in small frying pan over medium heat. Cook, stirring until golden brown, 8–10 minutes.

In same pan, stir coriander, cumin and fennel until slightly brown and fragrant. Transfer to 2nd plate to cool.

When everything is cool, finely chop (or pulse if you have a processor), transfer to mixing bowl.

In a spice grinder, pulse cumin, fennel and peppercorns till fine but not powdery.

Add spices, seeds, and salt to nuts. Cool.
Transfer dukkha to lidded glass jar.
Keeps for weeks.

Dukkha (2)

Dukkha also means *suffering*,
those afflictions pervading life
with impermanence and all that's unsatisfactory,
and I wonder at this linguistic convergence
of appetite and suffering.
Is *dukkha* the same as *acedia*, the sloth and torpor
considered vice by early clerics?
I look for busywork to distract me from the racket outside;
they're digging up the damn road again.
Fitful bursts of rain and wind sluice the window
where a close-flying gull has slung
a stream of guano—how do they do that? *Dukkha*.
Since I forgot my niece's birthday and my library books are overdue,
another dukkha, culinary, is an excellent avoidance activity.
Hauling out plates and pans a welcome distraction
from the world's delusion, greed and hatred, from armies of night
and from my own roiling resentments. Hazelnuts browning nicely,
and little plates of seeds line up politely for their turn.
Crunchy coriander (in its green youth, cilantro).
Earthy cumin, savoury and nutty, ancient as Egyptian tombs.
Fennel, my favourite, its anise tang doubled for this recipe.
It's calming, this staying in the moment; timing is all.
Small excitements as they come off the heat,
incense of accumulating fragrance. I've neither
burned my knuckles on the frying pan
nor sliced my fingers with my sharp sharp knife,
and for this moment, abolish the dukkha
of conspiracy delusions, drones bearing destruction,
and that heartbreaking huddle of tents
on Pandora Avenue.

Demeter Needs a Sabbatical

You always were a difficult child, wanted it both ways, wouldn't make your mind up, and look where that's got you. You've got a bit fat-headed, Miss *Queen of the Underworld*, and what am I, chopped liver? Let's have some respect, I've got connections too, you know—my brother Zeus for one. Well, yes, I'll admit he's also your father. It's true, all this family togetherness can get a bit much. And it's not as though I had a choice, so don't get all hoity toity Miss "*Just say no.*" And what is this, *blame the victim?*

Meanwhile, let's be pragmatic; it helps to have connections, powerful relations, or how would I have finagled your release? And it's not just connections; I've got my own turf, huge responsibilities, the whole damn earth's fertility, yes, all the crops and grain and fruits, including the pomegranate you're nibbling on, you greedy little gannet. All the armfuls of poppies, anemones, aconites you were picking when I'd told you to stay close to home. Who could blame Hades if he saw you then, so lovely, a fresh flower yourself. You might as well have posted it on Instagram!

Sorry, that was victim-shaming. And I made such a balls-up of the fertility thing once I knew you were lost to me. But I do miss you, my darling, it's so depressing, I just can't function when you're gone.

What on earth possessed you to eat those seeds? You knew they'd cancel your leave if you broke probation. Don't tell me you didn't want full release! You did! It never occurred to me that you'd cave! Didn't you ever think of your poor mother weeping all night, the thought of that brute crawling all over you? And crops dry as popcorn farts? I didn't raise you to be so irresponsible! Still, I have to admit, Hades is quite a hunk, all that dark, compressed, withheld Heathcliffian power, and he's besotted with you, I've heard. Well, I can hardly blame you. Quite fancied him myself. What, you're shocked? I'm not a Vestal Virgin, for Zeus' sake.

Oh Canada

The Canadian girl has settled in Barbados. She flies home for a cousin's wedding, new baby on her hip snuffling for the breast. On arrival, immigration officials divert, interrogate. There's nowhere to sit. The baby howls. Her breasts ache and leak. There's nowhere to sit. The baby is an illegal alien. Hours pass. The baby gets a three-week visa. On return, she lodges a complaint with the Canadian High Commission. The official says *Well, what do you expect when you turn your back on your country?*

It Isn't Nothing to Know Even One Moment Alive

It isn't nothing to know even one moment alive, but

isn't it a drag to keep interrogating the heart?

Nothing but myth around a four-chambered pump, delivering blood

to the right address. What I really want to

know is what your heart's made of. "Ice" thinks the disillusioned lover,

even "gold" dreams the hopeful one. "Tender" or "flinty," dithers the anxious

one. A heart murmur, in one case a lethal pounding of turbulent blood, in another, that

moment of the delicious prelude to lust in one another's arms, radiant,

alive, ready to take on the world.

Cyclamen

It all started in one of those self-indulgent moments of nostalgia I try to avoid. Early December with its driving rain and unbeautiful skies, raw knuckles and dripping noses its only promise. Not a chance of snow's lambent luminous light. But amid the root vegetables at the Rootcellar farmers' market, behold, a whole rack of cyclamen, delicate as hope, shone before me. It was kind of a mini-Damascus moment—you see what I mean by self-indulgent nostalgia. I bought a dozen and hurried home, forgetting the salami and compostable food bags I'd come for. Refined as they seem, cyclamen are ancient survivors, hardy in winter. They're found all over the place: Europe, Greece, the Caucasus, Iran, Somalia. Pliny the Elder called them *earth truffles*, even *amuletum* to counteract evil spells. In 1753, Linnaeus chimed in to offer a complicated phylogeny. I'm sure you wanted to know all this. Anyhow, I potted them out in terracotta planters, making a huge rainy mess with the bagged soil as CBC celebrated grace and innocence with *Jesu Joy of Man's Desiring*, the petals so glowing and translucent, a transcendental embodiment of Advent, I got all teary-eyed—I warned you of this. Then I wasted time looking for the salami I'd left behind. But everything isn't a metaphor. Not everyone loves cyclamen; the medieval English called it *swine-bread*, and apparently it poisons cats. Pigs find it a delicacy. The web explains how "growing points of the tuber become separated by shoulders of tissue and the tuber becomes misshapen." That's an ugly image, enough to make one check the mirror and consider an expensive skin cream. However, we've just had a killer week of unexpected Arctic outflow and even my cyclamen have succumbed, their limp bodies slumped over their terracotta deathbeds, like past-best chard and soggy Kleenex. "I see it's in my nature," I mourned to a girlfriend over the second glass of boxed wine and the rather stale end of the panettone, "I am the author of my own disappointments. And I don't even have the compostable bags I need to dump the cyclamen."

In This Morning's Podcast a Japanese Writer Speaks of Contemplative Focus,

suggests an assignment: to sit at a mirror for three hours,
silent, staring at one's own face.
Being a spiritual seeker, sort of,
but not up to the three hours, I'll try an hour,
hunker down at my IKEA BERGSBOP mirrored door
and set the timer. After, oh, I guess four minutes,
my back itches. Am I allowed to scratch? To fidget?
                                        The face, the face.
I settle into meditation mode, as nearly as I'm able
and eventually my mother's face surfaces.
Yes, and not for the first time. She's been emerging more lately.
Have I disappointed her?

Meanwhile a hummingbird at the window feeder,
Selasphorus rufus on the edge of my foveal vision,
that reptilian layer of sight, colourless awareness
of opportunity if you're a large snake,
danger if a small mammal.
The face. Eyes on the mirror, I observe
my irritation, frustration as the damn bird
flutters, pecks, twitches, breaks my concentration.
Aggressive little brute, if it was the size of a chicken,
that stiletto beak would be a yard long, could skewer you.

Back to my face, its two halves,
their duplicitous difference, left eye drooping,
something sly and shifty I am not pleased to see.
The right side my mother's, calmer, ingenuous even
and is that damn bird a spiritual test? Greedy
and selfish too, it'll attack another hummer
even if there are two feeders.
                                        The face, the face.
Ignore those iridescent flashes for memories
of our first sculpture project at art school,
a model skull and its overlaid muscles.
how we measured our own heads, fingered our boney jaws, cheekbones,
made faces in the mirror to ensure those thin clay slabs
became *frontalis*, our own frowny foreheads,
corrugator our wrinkled nose, that the muscles of mastication
met at the temporomandibular joint like our clay-streaked jaws,
so when we finished, we stood back like a dozen St. Jeromes,
staring into our own eye sockets.

Sometimes What I Feel Most Has No Name

as when I wrote a poem about *disambiguation*
before I found it is an incomprehensible technological term,
although it seems to express so beautifully
an indeterminacy of grief, unresolvable. *disambiguation.*

Likewise, *synovial.* Ah, *synovial*, doesn't it just slide? soothing
the fingers' synovial joints, their flexor tendons
oiling the machinery of the pianist's peerless precision.

and recently I found an excuse to use *temporomandibular.*

But what surfaces is a memory—was I eight or nine—
my weekly bus stop home after ballet, across the street
from an opaque black glass door marked *Executors.*
I misread ***EX****ecutors,* wept with horror
to think of those being executed
while I waited for the Fairfield bus home.

This afternoon is damp and chill, a nothing day
but my guilty pleasure is to pour
a shot of good Barbados rum and sip
while I meander my *Dictionary of Caribbean English Usage*,
a hefty seven hundred pages,
and I pour another two fingers of liquid gold,
revisit words I could not pack and bring home.
Sometimes what I feel most has no name
although in my Caribbean decades
my mouth grew languorous with vowels and
I often thought in dialect
so that one phone call, Mum said,
You're speaking very oddly, dear.

A folk wisdom that doesn't translate North:
Ev'ry skin-teet ent a smile warns me beware
of the flashy expensive dental smiles
of bank managers and car salesmen.

Politicians or children who *too own-ways*, or worse, *too hard-ears*
might find they *boil down to a small gravy*.
How better to acknowledge a well-mannered child
or a gracious woman than: *she got broughtupsy?*
She doesn't flaunt, show off, or *pompasett* about the place.

That tight knot of sorrow beyond words: a *grief-lump*.
And in a catastrophe, *yuh soul-case drop out*.

All afternoon words offered themselves to my displacement,
although sometimes what I feel most has no name.

Duplex: Parched

The opposite of love's not hate, it's just
indifference. Drought has shocked the salvia

into indigo flares. Drought's made the difference,
riots of cobalt across the parched field.

The heart's parched, a dry field rioting blues
that passersby evade, as though no harm

transpires from their evasive passage,
ignoring entropy, that random chaos.

Ignore entropy, seed chaos, the random
life where ardour fades to ennui in beds,

towns, nations. Life fades, arduous. Oppression
flourishes in these parched fields. Oh let them

green, let flourish. Let blue beauty flourish,
oppose indifference, love's unjust opposite.

Our Planetary Yard Sale

the world's multiple artifacts all go asunder
        rivers flood or drain   all weather dissipates
        as mud dries   cracks and crumbles   lands disintegrate
to sand and we subsist   in a penumbra

the world is tilting miles a year and so we gravitate
        live slantwise as we tumble upside down and slam
        as sure as continents will clash like dishpans
even stars   their half-life   half again   evaporate

incomprehensible   the black hole then inhales
        to splay us all in multiple dimensions   a fate
        we'd flee from   having to locate
amid the wreckage of our planetary yard sale

closing time folks   it's late   everything's sold
and sunset floods those tailings ponds with gold

Remote

It's not as if you knew them, she insisted,
I mean, there's no one you'd stop for, invite for coffee,
all bundled up, trudging in an off-putting way
as if there's somewhere they need to go,
but not in a hurry; they don't seem to have a sense
of purpose. The children whine,
tug at their mothers. The problem is
they just don't seem heroic, and you can only
stomach so much pathos.

And in the large gap between the buildings
the missiles took down, its pockets of fire
still flickering merrily, you can see through
to a landscape that's really quite lovely,
black soil springing green under the gold flood
of sunlight, a relief to take the mind off
unpleasant things as we switch to another channel
remembering tonight is
                                        Jeopardy.

Delusional

Let what happened   unhappen.

When I left his father, he cast me off. *Forever*, he meant.
On his birthdays I Google his address,
watch the screen in case he walks outside,
in case he pauses at his mailbox, turns his head
so if we meet again, I'll recognize him.

> On his birthday I Google his address,
> wait for his door to open. He stoops to stroke the cat,
> saunters to the mailbox. As graceful as his dad
> and even taller. His fine private smile
> travels the camera's eye to me.
> Is 23 years "forever"?

waiting without expectation,
remembering him an armful, a heartful,
my nut-brown boy, my dumpling, my jelly bean darling
crawling all over us, chortling, rumpling our sheets,
and how we all three laughed
when there was love between us.

> Surely the phone will ring   the voice I'd know
> in any airport, hospital, classroom, market
> *Hi Mum, I guess we should talk*

The perfect birthday gift is wrapped, sent,
returns, refused by recipient.

Oh he must have been away, how could I forget
he always wanted to see Machu Picchu
Look how he glows in the thin cold air
sunset gilding his face like an Inca mask
among the citadel's polished mysterious stones.
That's it   he's in Peru.

Still, on his birthday waiting for the email ping:
Mum, catch the early ferry from the Island.
I'll come down to meet you at Tsawwassen.

Conjuring a knock at my door   a replica
of his dad's shocking beauty. Greying temples.
He's as old as I was when we parted.
Hey Mum. We've wasted too much time.

He's taller than I recall.

My head fits exactly on his shoulder.

News of Graveyards Finds the Settler

but the vanished, the vanished beloved, o where?
Jane Hirshfield

Late cherry blossoms have drifted the road in a pink snow
and she's waiting for the finches' return.
She's partial to finches, gregarious and hectoring,
that bossy redhead and his dowdy missis,
how they push through the balcony's
unkempt rosemary, lavender, fescue, plants surviving
shreds of gales that push down whale-roads
where once great cedar canoes, hand-hewn,
traded on the Salish Sea, westward, far as T'Sou-ke.

Today is oddly tranquil. The wind has dropped,
its soundlessness a strangeness. Strident yells
from skateboard boys pierce the limpid air
like cries of battle. Finches add their heckling.
A day to drag the chair outside, crack a cold beer,
browse newspapers. Sun, silk on the skin.

The silky sun, the beer, the rustling paper, news . . .
It's sunny across Canada, that's nice, and
a crimp in the global economy,
its flow of toothpaste, toasters, trampolines,
and funds are being raised for homeless cats
and little leagues, and heritage flower gardens, and now
—can this be true?—
for ground-penetrating radar
to hone grief.

In the Kamloops valley, sun pours like honey
down slopes to a river that refracts
a periwinkle sky and a dark building.
The church is raising funds for restoration
of its stained-glass windows.
                                        Perhaps the Reconciliation Report—such heavy reading . . .
                                        Really, can't we just move on?

                                        No. No moving on.
Restitution is required, *greater than the settlement a city can*
pay a mother to stop crying,
shock and grief bequeathed to generations
until it had a familiar face:
            Children's voices, light as dust
            sift from the archive's heavy leaves,
            Oh   there you are.
                                    We remember
            porridge again, and not enough . . .
            Those priests   The strappings, and
            my best friend   gone,
            just gone one day.
                                    Remember us.

And radar, experts say, might not reveal
the actual remains at all:
uncoffined children lay in less impacted earth,
a shallow space; their small bones mouldered
Nothing left
            but a depression.

The Settler Digests Her Research

Evil is unspectacular and always human,
And shares our bed and eats at our own table,
And we are introduced to Goodness every day.
Even in drawing-rooms among a crowd of faults.
"Herman Melville," W.H. Auden

Among those King-and-country men, no malice intended,
and, along the Empire's ley lines no malign powers
among learned men, devout, respected, who
laid down paths of power straight as railroads.
No direct orders to trade small-poxed blankets,
which however cleared the way to blast straight
those winding roads to Caribou goldfields.
Tŝilhqot'in Chiefs resisted, came to negotiate,
instead were tried and hanged.
Evil is unspectacular and always human.

And even now, desked in glassy towers,
those in fine suits preside, suave and courteous,
signing codes and statutes, as their forbearers did,
to "kill the Indian in the child," shattering
families, submerging children in education's
brutal sanctifications, winning souls
of violated children who starved and wept,
were buried in innocent orchards. Now
each unquiet spirit visits our uneasy hearts
And shares our bed and eats at our own table.

Must history repeat? Tidy accountants,
their columned ledgers, grimoires of abuse
whose numbers don't add up. But random calamities
coalesce and focus with transplanted fury
to honour truth, let each small spirit rest.
Elders, Knowledge Keepers, gather harvests
of pain, of memory, voices that ring out like bells.
Ley lines are palimpsest, they limn ancient
navigations as hex and heal of history.
And we are introduced to Goodness every day.

Linguistic echoes stir, fragment by fragment,
lost words wash ashore on waves of Elders' memories
and once again, language lives. The longhouse rises, cedar-planked,
where all may meet once more with their regalia.
Voices are heard again in song, in story,
in poems, and in the halls of justice.
They are heard in the unceded city,
where sometimes on a still night, distant drums
pulse, beating under the wheeling stars
Even in drawing rooms among a crowd of faults.

The Weight of It

Beacon Hill Park   childhood walks
barred cage of the cougar
who paced and paced

adult years in another country
charting its way past
three centuries of wreckage
coralita's invasive lacey blooms
shrouding poinsettia hedges

that was then   now returned
to a matchbox-sized condo
seven floors up   its windows bring me
the Salish Sea's chameleon tides
indigo slump of the Sooke Hills
connective tangle of streets

the weight of seven floors
upon unceded territory
of those who lived   fished   worshipped   farmed
travelled their rich lives
before us

behind my building   the Gorge
surges from the harbour
up past dangerous narrows
pours back on outgoing tides

the weight of it
where once great seagoing canoes
who   can parse their passing . . .
the weight of it

evening sun turns
my balcony's blood-grass
to flame

Not Somewhere Else But Here

What good
is accuracy amidst the perpetual
scattering that unspools the world?
Ada Limón

Our local paper brings us news
of portable toilets removed
from the growing encampment of the unhoused
on the grounds that the toilets will be vandalized,
and that excess comfort will attract more layabouts.

At what point does taking a dump become excess comfort?
The West Coast's driving winds and slunging rain
cut to the bone long before freeze point.
What deficiency of imagination
considers a dumpster diet
(tossed pizza scraps, gnawed tacos, past-best pastry)
a culinary luxury?

This is not somewhere else but here.

The city fathers we elected are not monsters.
They golf on Fridays, keep their lawns mowed,
drive children to hockey. For evil to prevail,
a dismal absence of empathy and energy
will do the trick. Evil as banal as dishcloths.
They'd probably rather be washing their car
or playing billiards.
Still, they'll sign the requisite forms.

Next Day, There Was Nothing in the News

(after Ilya Kaminsky "In a Time of Peace")

I know it was a Friday because my poetry group meets on Friday.
Nice weather—venerable maples doing their October act,
kids kicking through heaps of leaves,
crows in the golden boughs making a racket.
The road hums with traffic all day; it's also a path
for wailing ambulances rushing over the blue bridge to the hospital.

But this afternoon, unusually quiet, just reading,
when a thunderclap *whump*, metallic clang,
we think *industrial accident*, rush to the window.
Large-scale construction is constant here,
                                                            and accidents happen
although it is otherwise a pleasant street.

A white BMW, crumpled on the sidewalk, surrounded
by three large unmarked black vans, eight or ten men
in riot gear, I guess, all padding, with the cutlery of enforcement,
a noir movie. Folks from the co-op across the street
stand on the stone wall with their phones out.

We watch. Watch
others watch.

Regulation police cars block traffic from either end
of our pleasant street while cops shout at the driver,
Then   more crashing noises and sounds like gun shots
and they wrench the door off,
                                                swing and fling a young man out
reminding me of rough schoolyard games when four of us would
swing and fling a classmate back and forth, but
we didn't sling them on the ground

as these cops do, so he slides across the pavement on his belly
and lies perfectly still, as though sun-bathing.
They kneel prayer-style around him. Or are they kneeling *on* him?
We're up-hill from them and cannot say for sure.
Then his leg twitches and they shout again,
and he wails *no no no* and begins to move and they prop him up
on the bus stop bench nearby. Things are quieter then
but they keep talking and he keeps crying, then
they're spraying him with something, exactly like
I spray my hair with Dove Style and Care Hairspray.

Did I mention the young man is Black?
Did I mention the police are not?
They put him into an unmarked van and drive away.

Another unmarked van drives up and men leap out with brooms and buckets,
sweep up all the broken glass like manic housewives.
The cop cars at the road's ends unblock traffic, which soon resumes.
A tow-truck appears, disappears the smashed car. On the boulevard,
golden maple leaves somersault in the evening breeze.

I'm in time to meet my poetry group at the Thai restaurant
and the conversation is all about copyright if I remember rightly.
I order pad thai, but do not enjoy it.

Does his mother wonder why he's late?
Put his dinner in the oven to stay warm?

Not Even on the Front Page

The article has already been relegated to page four.
Its grainy photograph shows workers
from some aid agency or other
ladling food from huge vats
that steam into the air like smoke.
Fronting the vats, a scrim of steam, a heavy chain-link fence,
chest-high, resisting the combined surge and press
of men. Each stretches forth a hand
clutching a dish, a pan, a pail, some manner of vessel.
Face gaunt, each distorted by a singular necessity:
survival. However momentary.
The crowd is a single beast, its many arms,
tentacles of famine, reach for life.

Surprisingly, a small girl has wormed her way to the front.
Her left hand clenches the chain-link fence;
her right grips the tin bowl she thrusts at aid workers,
one miniscule tentacle among many.
Her face no longer a child's face;
the famine beast has drawn her soft mouth
into the same rictus of terror and need
as the men around her. They mean her no harm
if indeed they notice her at all,
but if they could get inches nearer the food
they would stand on her head.

Pruned Before Flowering

You should have pruned that winter jasmine
right after flowering. Neglected so long,
it's lost its shape and intention, has a weeping habit
and who can blame it? Is there something unnatural
about gardening in pots seven floors above ground
when perhaps every root hair craves
to move deep into fecund earth?

The morning's windless, mist hanging above the bay.
No reason not to gather tools: secateurs, loppers,
a billhook, its design unchanged since the Bronze Age.
Cornus alba needs a full-crop cut to the ground. Your dreams
of next winter's new wood, its scarlet stems, take your mind

from the morning's news   doctors from one of the bombed hospitals
report that over a thousand children have had
one or more limbs amputated. A dreadful phrase, "one or more"
sounds casual, as though an afterthought, throwaway
and the Blue Cloak white fir, its silvery-blue pyramidal intentions
along its slightly weeping branches so neglected
it calls for surgical intervention, reminds you of

pre-Christmas trips with Dad
to his childhood farm, where his widowed mother
sent all five children, one by one
in the dawn milk-cart clop-clopping to the city high school.
The new farmer still welcomed your seasonal trudge
through snowy fields to cut a small fir tree for Christmas.

If you'd thinned the smoke-bush as you should,
such glory in its smoky pink influorescence!
Salix alba the white willow has reverted growth
that needs hard pruning, hopes for regeneration.
The bay laurel, dark and aromatic, forgiving;
you cut inside its body to hide the wounds,
one or more.

the broadcast was some time ago
perhaps the count is now   inaccurate

perhaps you'll dump the California lilac   its wind-scorched leaves
open branches   lax   beyond repair

doctors report inadequate supplies of analgesics

and oh   why weep   dead-head the lavender
sweep up   handfuls   their woodsy redolence
even the long stems   you cut back   to the joint

        their fragrance
                    why are you
                                weeping into your hands

Risking Delight

everywhere desolation

people of the book
all claim a loving god
yet spend centuries trying
to exterminate each other

and mothers with felt-tips   write
on the soft legs of their   children
their names that they may   be
known
after the inevitable

while here   the nearby inlet's shallows
percolate
an outgoing tide
that tugs with gentle insistence
        at sea grass flowing
                like hair of the drowned

yet bushes edging a trail
impenetrable as fairy tale thickets
are bejewelled with rosehips' scarlet lacquer
tangled with mahonia's pinnate leaves
their spiney leaflets and violet indigo berries
they call Oregon grapes here
so lavish   so prodigal

our neighbour harvested a bag
for preserves   brought us a jar brimming
tourmaline   sapphire   in the evening sun

how can the world insist this abundance?
how is it the stubborn heart leaps?
Elders warn a bounteous harvest
predicts harsh winter

yet who can listen unmoved to oboes and counter-tenors
and when a beloved friend returns, enters the room,
our hearts expand

we must risk delight   *we can do without pleasure*
but not delight
autumn's first Vs of *Branta canadensis*
practice their flight paths   soft creak of celestial wings
honking their long thrilling tremolo

our small exaltations
are surely defensible

Apostate

The vacuum left where once faith dwelt
feels like phantom limb. The godless, lapsed,

deprived of certainty in this life or the next
must search for beauty by the roadside

and such love as they can muster. Quiet joy
at living lightly on the land, and gratitude

for bees resonating in the lavender,
for the *Goldberg Variations*, for a perfect cappuccino.

Once a grumpy workshop poet snapped at me
Why do women always have to write of food?

But what's closer to the transcendental than
those tantalizing whiffs of garlic ginger thyme . . .

Perfection of the longing; consummation,
satisfaction doubled by the guest's delight.

Call It Grace

my mother's twin sister's three daughters
all gone in a decade   three-two-one
the youngest first   cancer
then the one my age   our shared birthday
her absurd misstep sprocketing the stairs
then   just a shock ago   the eldest of we four
a stroke   into that elsewhere.

lives enmeshed since   stories we whispered from
our shared bunks   our plots and plans   mirrored   braided

later   like fairytale quests   gadabouts to four countries
one   to Switzerland   love in the alpine chalet   ashes in the marital fireplace
one followed a dashing bassoonist to the far north
one to the US   lawyer in pinstripes   gin bottles hidden in the recycling
my own impetuous Caribbean quest   wanted   unwanted

now   how to reassemble
those remaining fragments of self
they'd brought into being   torn away
as I tumble into their empty spaces?

——

there are times as the year turns
when   if you climb the PKOLS' height at dawn
you can watch the sun rise and the moon set
at the same time   and the heart lifts into a great calm
where nothing is asked for   nothing lacking

what to call this gift beyond the fret and loss?
sun and moon on their reliable rounds
and the earth's momentary beauties
there is no word

call it grace.

A Life Full of Days

If you are lucky
You will die full of days

Arleen Paré

A Seashell Hiss, a Huge White Noise

(after Raymond Antrobus)

The moon's gone; it's dark now, silent
but for the seashell hiss that lives in my ear,
joined by a low-pitched drone overhead,
which grows, then fades. That'll be the morning's first seaplane,
its Inner Harbour landing. Soon,
grumble of lone engines: tired taxi drivers, early nurses,
farm deliveries, one by one, then
an overlapping susurration
until morning traffic
is a huge white noise that will stay
until I sleep again.

Waking, I fumble hearing aids.
I both dread and marvel at these tiny engines
that invade my ears' tympanic cavity, absorb their sounds
and, like medieval minstrels, convey them
through my ear's boney labyrinth,
the cochlea's elegant Fibonacci coils,
spiralling ribbons of hair cells
consigning electrochemical energy
down the auditory nerve
to my waiting brain.

Our neighbour practises her cello,
an avocation in pandemic solitude;
scales and simple exercises repeat.
I don't mind; it seems a colony of bees
hums our lathe and plaster wall,
or the stridulations of a gentle giant cicada.

At the museum's cetacean exhibit, touchable
silica whale brains, plaster skulls, braille signage.
A sightless woman strokes the tactile alphabet,
braille dots that whisper to her listening fingers
of whale migrations webbed with whale song,
those clicks, calls and whistles that cross oceans
to navigate migrations, or mate, or play with their young,
vibrate with sounds resembling cooing.

> *Gaudí believed in holy sound*
> *and built a cathedral to contain it*

wrote the deaf poet,
but, visiting Barcelona, added

> *I have not heard*
> *the golden decibels of angels.*

Word by Word

In the beginning was the Word, we're told,
but long before we reached those small meaningful units of language,
cosmic dust floated in an immensity of time and space
and *darkness was upon the face of the deep*
while the universe expanded and across the solar system patterns emerged
that would excite particle physicists, but that is getting ahead of ourselves.

Those charts from schooldays: our forebearers losing their fins
and climbing out of the slime, then upright hominids, but hunched and hairy.
Taller versions followed, more upright until the pinnacle, a well-muscled man.
Always a man, perhaps they hadn't encountered Eve's rib scenario,
or the beauty of natural law, like the Fibonacci spirals
of seedheads and pinecones, like nautilus shells and Renaissance paintings,
like the proportions of ancient Greece's Golden Mean,
and like the galaxies where all this started
and mitochondria-animated bacteria became capable of replication.
It's one theory of life's origin.
But wherever humans huddled, they all wanted to know
What does it mean?
And who is in charge?

Thus, religion and politics.
Along with cleverly chipped flints and so forth, humans need *words*.
You might argue other species communicate—
apes, elephants and whales have dialects, and even your dog
responds to the small narrative of *Sit. Good dog. Treat.*
But only we have metaphysical concerns and a cerebrum to give them meaning.
Oh praise the Grand Designer for our dominant left brain, our frontal lobes
our expressive utterances and decoding skills manifest in words.
Praise the tongue, lips, jaws turning vibrations into words,
Praise orbicularis oris, the kissing muscle.

Thus, neuroplasticity. So here we are, able to rewire our brains with words.
The brain's a tiny proportion of your body weight, but uses a fifth of what
you eat,
Thus, words, greedy words. You can contemplate your own stardust beginnings,
develop theologies or porn sites, write *Hamlet* or *Mein Kampf.*

One man said "I've been to the mountaintop" shortly before his murder.
One man said "Women, just grab 'em by the pussy" and ascended to great power.

Forgive Us Our Longing If It Intensifies

as we consider time, its flux in space.
Moon-cycles were ancestral clock enough to hunt
by day and rest by night, to plant and reap.
Ancient Australians trekked mountains, swamps
and deserts as long as their songlines.

But consider the heart, its fungible longings:
the birthday child's anticipation, endless.
The anxious lover's wait; the dilatory train.
But night's too short for Romeo, who heralded the morn
and youth, which surely was just yesterday?
My salad days, quoth Cleo, green in judgement.
And, *how many miles to Babylon?*

Consider the *doldrum* our Covidian unit of time
for pandemic sloth and torpor, days that last
forever, yet suddenly a year's gone. Or worse:
the extended pause between inhale, exhale,
family gathered round the deathbed, mournful,
not yet mourning. Not yet, not yet . . .

The Chinese *li*, archaic gauge of distance,
appraised both time and effort travelling A to B.
It's many *li* from joyful lusts of rowdy nights
to pension plans, support hose. And since
the public toilets closed: a *bladderful*'s the score.
Five *bladdersful* will last you from Victoria to Port Hardy,
but two are all you need to travel comfortably
from Tsawwassen ferry terminal to Hope.

Praise-Song For Minutiae of the Mutilated World

(after Adam Zagajewski)

My town snugs along the Island's south edge
neat as a foot tucks into its sock.
My town's mocked as a home for the newly wed and nearly dead,
which may also be fitting, since I am both.
But I praise its crusty beaches, washed-up logs scoured white as bone,
their stubborn press against the tides, their currents and cliffs,
their windsurfers and hang-gliders.

Praise the ancient souls of totems overseeing our public art,
the wacky life-sized blue bear, rainbow-hued chairs anchored to rocks,
gaudy glory of pianos beached above the shoreline,
painted with fish and flowers and planets,
where late at night I once drove a poet friend
following her triumphant reading,
and she played a thunderous Rachmaninoff
while waves crashed and shattered under the moon.

Praise webs of bike lanes, down which stream
seniors on e-bikes, toddlers in cargo wagons, bikes of course,
whole tribes of bikers in their space-age gear,
wheelchairs, skateboards, wagons, and the odd unicycle.

Praise proliferations of Little Free Libraries,
over 700 last count, scattered across parks and driveways,
through neighbourhoods, gates and fields, crammed in alleys.
Praise their builders, architects of miniature cabins, huts, homes,
some replicas of owners' houses. Some echo churches,
castles of Byzantine complexity; one surely channelled
mad Ludwig of Bavaria.

Praise minutiae of the darkening world, tattoos of young baristas,
the way passengers on the #14 bus move courteously aside,
help with strollers and walkers.
Praise the teen who raced after me
with my forgotten toque.
Praise those calling *Thank you, Driver*
as they exit the rear door.

An Exuberance of Apples

1.

coastal cottage rental   tide-heaving waves   fearsome
gusts shudder rain across windows   night moiling black
we light candles   try to keep the fire going
grill cheese sandwiches on the old wood stove
oh savoury salvation   delectable   snuggled
on the sagging couch under the old HBC blanket
how sapid   slabs of Manchego   Camembert   Parmesan
and the crisp slice of their apple consorts   Gala   Ambrosia
that little bite of resistance   so piquant
as the heat rises   the melting   stormed cabin shaking
and shaking   but we don't notice
one sandwich we'll find in the morning
squashed flat under the cushions

2.

so finally we sit up   cross-legged
on the ravenous sheets   down the remains
of the apple pie   good so good   pastry flaking
so tender from its rolling and folding   rolling and folding   flaking
on our moist skin   delicate *pâte feuilletée*
apples   sweet tart in their pastry monstrance
slightly crisp   tongues and teeth work   their juices
syrupy trickle   your cinnamon-scented skin
lick up every drop   every crumb

3.

bundling into the narrow hall   arms full of market bags
we stop to kiss   squashed against the door
and the bag dumps apples everywhere
laughing so hard we slide down the wall
as apples rollick all over the floor
where we lie until they calm down
but I bang my elbow something awful on the coat stand
which falls   Stygian darkness covering us
with loden coats and puffy jackets as
we consider the apple
for Aphrodite, love's symbol
for people of the book   temptation and downfall
for the Greeks   sliced apple as vulva   fertility
but the judgement of Paris   didn't end well

The Excellence of Bears

(With apologies to *Hamlet*)

1.

consider the excellence of bears, *paragon of animals,*

how mighty in power   how swift sleek their bulk

how discerning of territories, of their comfort and safety, of their inhabitants

how learned of creaturely ways   of woods and waters
connoisseur of roots grass berries insects nuts fish

how adroit of movement to scale trees   to protect young

in form and function how express and admirable
in playfulness and delight to cool off in lakes
in deftness to hook salmon from frothing shallows

how mythic their place in all nations   warriors and spirit animals
transformations   Haida Bear Mother Taan AwGa   human/bear cubs
massive in skill and skull   Norse *bjorn*-inspired Berserkers

2.

oh *Ursus americanus kermodei*
how I could join those bearpeople
stroke glossy coats of many layers
shorter insulated layer for warmth
waterproof layer for protection
with them burrow in for hibernation   scrunch and nestle
cram in lavish excess of nuts berries roots
(perhaps not the larvae and pupae)
magnificent hyperphagia   gorge and fatten for winter
and then hibernation through the cold and dark

how I could wallow in that fur carapace
curl into dens through lightless times
the wonder of that long hibernation
metabolic dormancy   slowing blood
until green up   waking hot-blooded   ravenous
what dreams might come   what poems

White Crane Spreads Wings

last sailing   the island ferry   almost empty
throbs through slate-dark air   juddering
its few travellers   slumped or snoozing
small town a pinprick light-line on the horizon

rust and creak of churning blades below
only the bow window's oily ribbons of light
coat corrugated breakers ahead,
                                        dissolve into dark

my life's mid-point now far behind
nightfall   tides   the ferry's throb

from the corner of my eye
                                  another rhythm

wavering reflections on the black window
a tall woman   white-haired
she moves through *dan yu*   and my body remembers
        white crane spreads wings
and my hands twitch
        grasp bird's tail   strum the pei pa

her grace and pivot absorb night and tides
till my body rises without volition   it can
ward off monkey. It can
deflect
      chop
            parry
                  lift tiger to mountain.
It can   *part wild horse's mane*

our twinned reflections' echo
as we
        move hands like clouds

as we pull into the sleeping port and
        push needle to sea bottom.

Galactic Scripture

In grade three, Miss Hunter closed the blinds,
used an orange, a lemon and a flashlight
to teach us eclipses and the size of the universe.
She enchanted us with stars named after Greek gods
in our *Golden Book of Myths and Legends*,
so it was not a stretch to revere an in-charge creator
and Yes Jesus Loves Me.

Though I'm long lapsed, oh, lapsed beyond repair,
at times I've been nostalgic for that cozy certainty
recently triggered by James Webb's telescope,
its galactic images so lavish and painterly
they rival Van Gogh's *Starry Night*.
It's enough to make you fall on your knees.

I've tried to comprehend those distances: vast
cosmic islands of stars, gas and dark matter
held together by gravity. Inside them, glowing gases
spin new stars, and galaxies, spiral, elliptical, irregular –
but they lost me at the black holes and quasars.
Andromeda, a barred spiral galaxy, is endearingly humanized,
being named after an Ethiopian princess
chained to a rock for a sea serpent, but rescued by Perseus,
our old friend from the *Golden Book*.

How did the camera, mere tool, penetrate
the enormity of those spaces?
(I don't like that term *penetrated*,
find it hostile and aggressive, although it seems
to be used for any new scientific discovery.)
How to imagine, let alone measure the dimensions of
galaxies containing billions of stars, beyond comprehension
though their photographs, galactic scripture,
limn immeasurable beauty.

I cannot picture the God of Old or New Testament,
nor Michelangelo's muscular, white-robed Creator
as lord of this domain.
But I open to unknowing; there are mysteries remaining far beyond
our puny human brains to understand
and to these I namaste, I hold up my hands, I say
Holy, holy, holy.

These Steady Accrections

(Homage to Patrick Lane, 1939–2019)

These steady accretions, yet allowing them to stay
as you stay with music after music plays.
Oh word-slinger, minstrel, polyglot, bard,
you who so utterly inhabited yourself
yet found room for infinite kindnesses,
who taught us to hear music in poems
and then to make our own:

How you hammered in your lexicological smithy,
you verse-maker, cadence-meister, how ruthless
you pushed us steadfast down our own paths
not yours, so we were not little Patricks.
Your insistence a poem's power grows
from passionate detachment.
Woe to we who wallowed in sentiment and all the feels,
whose wounds would know that sharp red pen.

May the craft of our own poems be witness

because sock-footed poets in the retreat room
would speculate on the splendour of your socks,
because you would cook wokfuls of prawns in garlic,
count out six per poet, punctilious,
because you made us howl at your feigned astonishment
as women debated incomprehensible urges
like taking an afternoon to organize the sock drawer.
Because you would cradle an errant house-bound spider,
deposit it gently on leaf or branch.

Oh   you have gone into your own silence
and we remain, honing our poems, muttering *what would Patrick say . . .*
murmuring our doxology
passionate detachment, passionate detachment.

Loving Everything that Increases Me

By a church in Metchosin, you write, the Erythronium bloom
but here, the sky above this lake is palest blue,
sunlight chill and brassy. On the far shore, mountains
that last summer seemed all mist and tissue
rear up, their iron-dark slopes blazed white
with clear-cuts, snow-burdened. Spring is late here,
but naked branches nubbed with promised growth,
and cherry trees, pollarded, their doubled row
a blossom tunnel, bridal, where I strolled this morning,
loving everything that increases me.

Far from here, you read, perhaps, or put on opera,
or curl beneath the quilt in sleep, or dream,
or toss and turn, uneasy, missing me. Perhaps you miss
lying in my arms as, over rooftops, the moon rises
amid rivered stars, faithfully and on schedule.

The Blessings of Water

(after Arleen Paré)

although we transmogrify marshlands with concrete rebar gunk
although we burn the lungs of the planet from Amazon to boreal North
it is a blessing that water gathers its gravities
lays upon the earth a shining cloak
that clings though the globe's great spindle turns

that it gathers to find its level fills every cavern every fissured deep
tops up crater and ravine and mineshaft each burrow and den
every grotto ossuary and crypt
that it spreads upon each ocean every lake each fiord loch and lagoon
each cistern every rice paddy and marsh

it is a blessing of water that it spills from high places to flatten its watery highways
its capillaries of creek and runnel churning with lives finned and webbed
bless the earth's pulsing tides and currents linking night to day
as our own veined bodies our own pulses systole diastole
bless the abiding rain and fog and mist
that quicken springing crops unfurling greens of seasons in their order
this too the earth's pulse our bodies echo

that it sustains the earth's goodly creatures nugget of the hummingbird's heart
thrumming 1000 times a minute the blue whale's massive grace
great chambers of its heart its slow beat audible for miles
ocean-wide resonance of its songs

so we call these settled waters *bodies* of water   as we are creatures of water
our blood and plasma   organs and sweat and urine   *our* bodies of water
joined as all the oceans adjoining   all the lakes and rivers that web the earth
bless water's reflections   that instruct us in exact and vivid appearances
bless its refractions   that remind us all we see is distortion
bless the clear cold water   of childhood's summer cabin
its little squeaky kitchen pump   bless the deep wells
and bless the tired wells   drying in drought   bless their low scummed level
and queues of women with pots   with buckets   patient   bless them

Its Miraculous Blue

It comforts them to think of the aging
as serene, equanimous, resigned, and
grateful for the *having-had.*
Having had their share of good times,
leaving with a peaceful sigh   a blessing
for relatives who'll circle the tidy death bed,
glancing at smart phones, wonder how long . . .
they've kids to pick up, golf, dry cleaning . . .
They don't yet understand
that no one
wants to go home from the party.

We who have skin in the game
once thought so too, but
no longer tell ourselves
that the stop sign at the end of the road
is a red party balloon.
(Even fish out of water know
to thrash with every fibre of being,
to gulp the poisonous air
against *the dying of the light*)

And the young, believing themselves
forever shielded by their supple muscles,
snug in their smooth smooth skins,
cringe, say *TMD* to hear that
we aged have never felt more passionate.

We turn music way up, sprinkle excessive
cardamom, ginger, habanero pepper.
We savour wine corks, read away insomniac nights,
fold friends tight in our hearts, and
yes, yes, lovers too.
The razor's edge of immanent loss
grows our appetites, voracious.

How every step along that road glows,
radiant with counterpoint
of finches' warble, swallow's liquid *slip-lip*.
The urgent grass undulating.
Chicory bloom flooding the verges
                                                  with blue, its miraculous blue.

One Day One of Us

I sometimes wonder if I dreamed climbing that stairwell

its three-floor glass wall black with night where

outside bamboo plantings   those green blades metallic under nightlights

swished and scritched the panes   your slow steps descending as I climbed

distant cleaners trolleying   I hardly knew you   inexplicable

we must have found words   an enchantment   students long dispersed

someone distant   called to someone   who has the damn keys

and if we'd known   the coming chaos   would I have not fallen out of my world

would I have not said   I packed my toothbrush   would I have not fallen

into your arms   all these years   although I know that

one day one of us   will wake reaching across an empty bed

before we remember

Each Swift-Winged Glad-Glowing Day

(after e.e. cummings' "i thank You God for most this amazing")

the old prayer begins *give us this day*
and I *am* grateful for this day, glad to reach
the first day of my 82nd year   a dawn softly grey
and grateful that we waken near a beach

where sound-absorbing fog blankets swells of surf
to tide-silk   its edges quiet-nibbling ribbed sandtracks
while sunrise gongs behind the mist   and burns it
to clarity   so   water-strider-quiet we take kayaks

up the glass-grey tide   swoop-and-calling birds start
their day   great blue heron   we glide gingerly
past his morose hunch   barnacled log   his stab and dart
to gulp some tiny silver agony

oh abundance   even this   and the time
we have left   each swift-winged glad-glowing day chimes

Acknowledgements

Writing is a lonely process, but it survives and thrives amidst the BC coast's and islands' generous allotment of poets and poetry organizations.

Huge gratitude to Harbour Publishing's team, who guided me through the complicated publishing process so adeptly and with such kindness and clarity.

I'm so thankful for the intense creative immersion and invaluable mentorship of annual poetry retreats first led by Patrick Lane (1939–2019,) and then by Lorna Crozier. (In recent years also offered by Laura Apol.)

Thanks unbounded to my "home" reading series, Planet Earth Poetry. PEP has livened Victoria's Fridays with its weekly open mics and readings for nearly thirty years!

Thanks to the small intimate poetry groups who workshop and critique and support: Our stalwart monthly Waywords, with thanks to Barbara Black, Barbara Pelman, Cynthia Woodman-Kerkham, Anne Hopkinson, David Pimm, Pam Porter. To Quattro, workshopping ongoing projects, with Terry Ann Carter, Kate Braid, Leah Fowler. To Modpo for discussions of contemporary poetry with Katrin Horowitz, Joy Huebert, Ulrike Narwani, Leah Fowler. Hugs to you all.

To poet buddies Susan Braley, Anne Hopkinson, and Arleen Paré, I'm so appreciative of many vibrant productive poetry conversations and a great deal of caffeine. Praise be!

My whole heart's gratitude to my in-house techie, listener, editor, and spouse: thank you Leah Fowler. Your invisible work is in this book; its maker sustained by your ongoing love and encouragement.

I gratefully acknowledge that I live and write in view of the Sooke Hills and the Salish Sea, on the unceded traditional territory of the lək̓ʷəŋən Peoples of the Songhees and Esquimalt Nations.

Endnotes

Epigraph

"where are we moored? . . .," Adrienne Rich, Part XI "One night on Monterey Bay the death-freeze of the century," *An Atlas of the Difficult World.*

That Sensible Planning-Ahead Thing

Section epigraph

"Did they wonder: How did we come to this?" Wendy Donawa, "Leaving Pendegast."

That Sensible Planning-Ahead Thing

Eros: Greek god of love and sexual desire.

Thanatos: Greek personification of Death, bringing the souls of the dead to Hades.

The Wolf in Me

Statistics of "Donawa" name from 2010 US Census.

Small Boys in Sailor Suits

In pre-antibiotic times, with their high rates of infant and child mortality, a child was not infrequently given the name of a previously deceased sibling. The sailor suit boy is the second Gordon.

Gemini Terribiles

gemini terribiles: Terrible twins.

Shame

"Look thy last on all things lovely" and "Till to delight / Thou have paid they utmost blessing," Walter de la Mare, "Fare Well." http://www.poemtree.com/poems/FareWell.htms

That Conjured Last Day

Charon: a minor god, ferrying the souls of the dead across the Styx, river of death.

"little cakes," D.H. Lawrence, "The Ship of Death," *Last Poems by D.H. Lawrence*. New York: The Viking Press, 1933.

Scorch of Time

"The righteousness I had / before the scorch of time" and "I miss who I was," Ada Limón, "Salvage," *The Hurting Kind*. Minneapolis, Minnesota: Milkweed Editions, 2022.

"impatience bows in service to a larger story," Alison Luterman, "Because even the word obstacle is an obstacle."

Yourdailypoem.com. https://www.yourdailypoem.com/listpoem.jsp?poem_id=385

The poem first appeared in *The Sun Magazine*, January 2010.

Between Ground and Feast

Section epigraph

"Between / the ground and the feast is where I live now," Ada Limón, "Not the Saddest Thing in the World," *The Hurting Kind.*

The Time of Falling Apart

Garry oak: *Quercus garryanna*: a protected oak species found in the Pacific Northwest.

grisaille: a popular Renaissance painting technique entirely in black, white and greys.

Duplex: Glean

The duplex form, with its ghazal-like leaps, is an invention of Jericho Brown's: 14 lines, like a sonnet, in 7 couplets. The 2nd line of each couplet is echoed in the first line of the next couplet.

The first line is repeated in the last line, like a pantoum.

Jericho Brown, *The Tradition.* Port Townsend, WA: Copper Canyon Press, 2019.

Online Poetry Workshop in the Plague Year

"poignancy of his gopher-skin cloak"

Mummified body of a young hunter found in a northern BC glacier in 2008. Named Kwaday Dan Ts'inchi ("long-ago person found"), he died an estimated 300 years ago. He had tools and was wearing a cloak finely stitched from 95 gopher skins.

Pandemic Blues

"staring into the refrigerator / as if into the place where answers are kept," Steven Dobyns, "How to Like It," *Velocities: New and Selected Poems 1966–1992.* Penguin Books, 1994.

Lessons from the Silver Screen

"I grew up with movies that taught me the meek," Amber Dawn, first line from *My Art is Killing Me and Other Poems.* Vancouver BC: Arsenal Pulp Press, 2021.

Vermeer's *Milkmaid*

"Desire pervades everything, nothing human can be cleansed of it" is a prose quotation from Anne Michael's novel *Held*, Toronto: McClelland & Stewart / Penguin Random House Canada, 2023.

The ingredients of many artist's materials, especially minerals, were often highly poisonous.

Oh Canada

At the time of this event, children of Canadian men and Barbadian women could acquire Canadian citizenship: children of Canadian women and Barbadian men could not.

It Isn't Nothing to Know Even One Moment Alive

"but it isn't nothing / to know even one moment alive," Ellen Bass, "Any Common Desolation"; the poem also provides the structure (first word of each line) for this acrostic poem.

Ellen Bass, *Indigo*. Port Townsend, WA: Copper Canyon Press, 2020.

Remote

Maternity hospital #3, Mariupol, bombed by Russian Armed Forces March 9, 2022.

News of Graveyards Finds the Settler

Epigraph: "but the vanished, the vanished beloved, o where?" Jane Hirshfield, "Poem with two Endings," *Given Sugar, Given Salt*. New York, NY: HarperCollins, 2001.

In June 2021, ground-penetrating radar confirmed the burial of 215 children on the grounds of the Kamloops Indian Residential School. Shockingly similar scenarios have been subsequently found in virtually all the government-administered Indigenous residential schools.

"Greater than the settlement / A city can pay a mother to stop crying," Jericho Brown, "Bullet Points," *The Tradition*. Port Townsend, Washington: Copper Canyon Press. 2019.

The Settler Digests Her Research

Ley lines: straight alignments drawn between historic structures and prominent landmarks, often interpreted to have spiritual or occult significance.

Tsilhgot'in: Chilcotin. The so-called Chilcotin War (1864) marked the intrusion of road-building crews into Tsilhgot'in lands to construct a shortcut to the Caribou goldfields. The Tsilhgot'in, already decimated by the 1862 smallpox epidemic, were facing starvation, and in face of several acts of ill faith, attacked both road gangs and settlers. What they saw as an act of war was construed as murder, and the negotiating chiefs were hanged.

The phrase "kill the Indian in the child" has been attributed, some say wrongly, to poet and career civil servant Duncan Campbell Scott.

"Voices are heard . . . in the halls of justice": "Calls to Action," *Final Report of the Truth and Reconciliation Commission of Canada*. Toronto, ON: James Lorimer & Company Ltd., 2015. pp. 319–37.

Not Somewhere Else but Here

Title from Adrienne Rich's, "What Kind of Times Are These?" *Collected Poems: 1950–2012*. New York: W.W. Norton, 2016.

Retrieved February 24, 2025 from https://www.poetryfoundation.org/poems/51092/what-kind-of-times-are-these

"What good / is accuracy amidst the perpetual / scattering that unspools the world," Ada Limón, "It's the Season I Often Mistake," *The Hurting Kind*.

Next Day, There Was Nothing in the News

"We watch. Watch / others watch," Ilya Kaminsky's "In a Time of Peace," *Deaf Republic*. Minneapolis: Graywolf Press, 2019.

Retrieved from Academy of American Poets. https://poets.org/poem/time-peace

Risking Delight

"We must risk delight. We can do without pleasure, / but not delight," Jack Gilbert, "A Brief for the Defense," *Refusing Heaven*. New York, NY: Alfred A. Knopf, 2009.

Apostate

". . . search for beauty by the roadside/and such love as they can muster." Plagiarized from one of my own old poems: "Ru Pu Paints Zhong Kui the Demon Queller on a Mule," *Thin Air of the Knowable*. London, ON., Brick Books.

A Life Full of Days

Section epigraph

"If you are lucky / you will die full of days," Arleen Paré, "Etel Adnan 1" in *Time Out of Time*. Qualicum Beach BC: Dagger Editions, 2022.

A Seashell Hiss, a Huge White Noise

The deaf poet: Raymond Antrobus.

"Gaudí believed in holy sound / and built a cathedral to contain it" and "I have not heard / the golden decibels of angels," Raymond Antrobus, "Echo," *The Perseverance*. London, UK: Penned in the Margins, 2018.

Gaudí: Catalan architect of Barcelona's enormous Sagrada Família Cathedral, now a UNESCO World Heritage site.

Word by Word

"I've been to the mountain top." Martin Luther King's speech to the Memphis Sanitation Strike Workers, urging non-violent protest a day before his murder on April 4, 1968.

Transcript of *I Have a Dream* speech: https://www.npr.org/2010/01/18/122701268/i-have-a-dream-speech-in-its-entirety.

Forgive Us Our Longing If It Intensifies

The *doldrum* and the *bladderful* are measurements that exist only in my imagination, but the *li* is real.

An apologetic nod to Shakespeare for Romeo's aubade and Cleopatra's salad days.

The nursery rhyme "How many miles to Babylon," like many nursery rhymes, has roots in darker and more adult or political themes. (Babylon has long been a symbol of sin to Christians, and the rhyme also ended up in Joyce's *Finnegans Wake*.)

Praise-Song For Minutiae of the Mutilated World

Adam Jagajewski, "Try to Praise the Mutilated World," *Without End: New and Selected Poems*, translated Clare Kavanagh, Renata Gorczynski, Benjamin Ivry, C.K. Williams. New York: Farrar, Straus & Giroux, 2003.

The Excellence of Bears:

Berserkers: pre-medieval Norse warriors who fought in a trance-like rage, thought to have a bear's strength and wildness.

Taan AwGa Bear Mother: Haida myth of a young woman who offends and is captured by the bears, eventually marrying one and bearing twin cubs. In later life mother and sons return to her village in human form.

Italicized phrases from Shakespeare's *Hamlet*.

Galactic Scripture

James Webb Telescope: the largest telescope in space. Its high sensitivity instruments allow it to view objects too old, too distant, or too faint for the Hubble Space Telescope.

These Steady Accretions

Homage to Patrick Lane (1939–2019), for whose generous mentorship and rigorous encouragement I will always be grateful.

Patrick Lane, "These steady accretions, yet allowing them to stay / as you stay with music after music plays," *The Bare Plum of Winter Rain*. Madeira Park: Harbour Publishing, 2000.

The 'collect' (pr. COLL-ekt) is an ancient petitionary prayer form some modern poets have adapted. Its five parts are:

(1) address to a being or Being,
(2) something descriptive about the being,
(3) petition(s),
(4) benefit or result,
(5) words of praise/amen.

Loving Everything That Increases Me

"Loving everything that increases me," Raymond Carver's poem "where water comes together with other water," *Where Water Comes Together with Other Water: Poems*. New York, NY: Vintage / Random House, 1986.

The Blessings of Water

After Arleen Paré's "These Are the Trials of Water," *He Leaves His Face in the Funeral Car*. Halfmoon Bay, BC: Caitlin Press, 2015.

Its Miraculous Blue

"Rage, rage against the dying of the light," Dylan Thomas' villanelle, "Do Not go Gentle into That Good Night." Originally published in 1951 in the *Botteghe Oscure*, a literary journal in Rome.

Each Swift-Winged Glad-Glowing Day

After e. e. cummings' "i thank You God for most this amazing," originally published in *Xaipe*. New York: Oxford University Press, 1950.